Betty White

COLLECTOR'S EDITION

By Deborah Hopkinson
Illustrated by Margeaux Lucas

A GOLDEN BOOK • NEW YORK

rhcbooks.com
Educators and librarians, for a variety of teaching tools, visit us at RHTeachersLibrarians.com
Library of Congress Control Number: 2022936275
ISBN 978-0-593-64768-4 (trade)
MANUFACTURED IN CHINA
10 9 8 7 6 5 4 3 2 1

Betty White was born on January 17, 1922, in Illinois, and grew up in California. Betty and her parents enjoyed hiking, nature, and animals. She was an only child, but she got to be a sister to lots of cats and dogs.

Betty always felt surrounded by love, and she spent her long and remarkable life giving that love back—to family and friends, to audiences, and to animals in need.

When she was young, Betty wanted to be a forest ranger or a zookeeper. But those careers weren't open to girls at that time.

Luckily, Betty had other passions. She loved to write, sing, and perform in plays. Early on, she set her heart on being an actress.

Betty graduated from high school in 1939. Two years later, America entered World War II. Betty wanted to help in any way she could, so she volunteered to drive a truck carrying supplies to soldiers stationed in California.

After the war, Betty set out to follow her dreams. She knew getting into show business wouldn't be easy, but she was ready for anything!

Betty was bright, talented, beautiful, and funny, but she had to work hard to find jobs. She acted in local theaters and got small roles in radio commercials.

Betty wanted to be on television. Back then, there were far fewer TV shows, TV stations, and TV jobs than there are today. But Betty's hard work paid off. In 1949, she got her first full-time job, as the host's helper on a daytime show called *Hollywood on Television*. (Later, she became the host herself!)

Today, most television actors memorize lines from a script someone else has written. Not Betty! She had to think on her feet, or "wing it," in front of a live studio audience. And there were no breaks because Betty and the other actors performed in the commercials, too.

That meant Betty was in front of the camera five and a half hours a day—six days a week! Could she do it? You bet she could! Betty learned a lot and loved every minute. And viewers adored her from the start.

Television grew and changed quickly, and so did Betty. She became one of the first female producers in Hollywood when she cofounded Bandy Productions, named after one of her dogs.

On Betty's first show, she had interviewed movie stars. Now Betty and her business partners decided to make a situation comedy, or a sitcom, about made-up characters. It was called *Life with Elizabeth*.

And this time, Betty was the star!

Betty always believed in being fair to all people. In 1954, when she hosted a variety show—with skits and musical guests—TV stations in some parts of the country didn't want to air it. They didn't like that a Black dancer, Arthur Duncan, was in the cast. They wanted Betty to fire him.

Any kind of prejudice made Betty mad.
Arthur stayed on the show and had a long,
successful career. And Betty and Arthur
remained friends through the years.

As a girl, Betty had enjoyed playing games with her mom and dad—and beginning in the 1950s, she became a popular guest on television game shows!

Betty's quick wit charmed everyone, including one special man, Allen Ludden, the host of a show called *Password*. Allen and Betty fell in love.

They married in 1963, and Betty became stepmom to his three children. Betty and Allen lived happily together until Allen died in 1981.

Life wasn't easy for Betty after Allen's death, but staying busy helped her cope.

Betty liked new challenges and taking on different roles. She studied, prepared, and worked hard. That's one reason she was one of the most successful television stars in history!

Betty is especially known for acting in two popular, long-running TV shows—*The Mary Tyler Moore Show* and *The Golden Girls*. She won Emmy Awards for both.

Betty was honored many times. In 1995, she was inducted into the Television Academy Hall of Fame. Was Betty ready to stop working then? No way! She wrote books about her life and kept acting in movies and on television.

SATURDAY NIGHT LIVE

At age 88, Betty became the oldest host of the comedy show *Saturday Night Live*. Betty received an Emmy for her performance—another honor in her long list of awards.

Even with her busy acting career, Betty always
found time for animals. She supported the Los Angeles
Zoo for many years and helped raise money to improve
animal habitats and save endangered species, like the
California condor.

Betty was also lucky enough to meet some creatures that were just as famous as she was, including Koko the gorilla. Koko knew more than a thousand words in sign language. In fact, Koko gave Betty the name Lipstick. She made the sign for the word whenever Betty came to visit.

Along with helping wild animals, Betty supported groups that rescue pets, study animal health, and train guide dogs.

Betty had loved cats and dogs since she was little. "I grew up with pets. In our house, they were more than pets—they were members of the family."

When she was 89, Betty adopted Pontiac, a golden retriever who hadn't been able to finish his guide dog training.

Betty's kindness and talent brought joy to millions. Her passion for helping animals inspired others to do the same.

Betty passed away on December 31, 2021, just weeks before what would have been her 100th birthday on January 17. Fans everywhere donated money in her honor to animal rescues and shelters. How that would have made her smile!

Betty loved to make the world happy. No wonder people and animals loved her right back.